Corn[wall's]
Rotten MPs

Paul White

Bossiney Books • Exeter

Some other Bossiney titles you may find interesting

First published 2024 by
Bossiney Books Ltd, 68 Thorndale Courts, Whitycombe Way,
Exeter, EX4 2NY
www.bossineybooks.com
© 2024 Paul White
ISBN 978-1-915664-35-8
Cover illustration by permission of Look and Learn – Historical Picture Archive
Printed in Great Britain by Deltor, Saltash, Cornwall

Rotten boroughs and pocket boroughs

Before 1832 Cornwall was famous for its 'rotten boroughs' – parliamentary constituencies where a seat in parliament could be bought. London with a population of 1,500,00 in 1831 had 6 MPs; Cornwall, with a population of 300,000 had 42: Birmingham, Manchester and Leeds none. This was obviously totally undemocratic (but then, the ruling class at that time thought 'democracy' treasonable) and it was a splendid opportunity for genteel corruption.

There was a theoretical difference between a 'rotten borough' and a 'pocket borough'. Pocket boroughs were in the pocket of a particular patron and had been created with that in mind. The power was then inherited through the family – or sold. Rotten boroughs were places which had been larger and/or more important in their day, but had ceased to deserve electoral borough status. In fact most of the Cornish boroughs described in the early 19th century as 'rotten' were already too small at the time they were created to have deserved the franchise, so technically they were pocket boroughs.

Election day

There was no secret ballot. Every voter had to show publicly who he voted for, and face the consequences. In Cornwall in 1831 just 9% of adult males were eligible to vote. (A very, very small number of women with property were also allowed to vote: it was the 'Great' Reform Act of 1832 which actually *excluded* all women from voting!) Of that 9%, many were tenant farmers. Landowners made it clear to their tenants who they should vote for if they wanted their tenancy renewed. Some estate archives still contain lists of who the tenants voted for at particular elections – and it is almost always for a single candidate.

Where voters were less under threat from their landlord, as in towns (though in some towns the corporation dictated the choice), elections were contested, and a carrot was needed instead of a stick. Bribery might take the form of a sumptuous feast, or sometimes of actual cash. Voters in Grampound boasted that they had received 300 guineas per man.

In most constituencies, one or two local landowners ('patrons') effectively chose the MPs themselves – but quite often their choice was as a favour to persons even higher in society, or in return for a remuneration or favour. Uncontested elections were very common, because fighting against the patrons' choice was likely to be a waste of money.

Who were the candidates?

MPs did not receive a salary – though they might well hope to receive perks. Across the country as a whole, many candidates were sons of aristocratic or upper gentry landowners. As MPs they would spend part of their time (usually a small part) in Westminster getting to understand the political system, meeting people in power, and becoming part of a network of mutual favours. 'You vote for my Bill, and I'll recommend you for that job' – a job which might be a sinecure, where the office holder received a good salary and the actual work was done by an ill-paid clerk. This was before the days of a professional Civil Service. Quite a few young MPs were in effect serving an apprenticeship prior to membership of the House of Lords.

Another kind of candidate was a man who had already made his name and fortune in a different activity, and wanted to play an active part in politics. Sir Francis Drake was one such. These people might well be prepared to pay a goodly sum to become the preferred candidate for a rotten or pocket borough. Until 1821, when Grampound was disenfranchised for corruption, Cornwall had 44 MPs; then there were 42 until 1832. Because of the large number of Cornish seats,, there were fewer locals putting themselves forward, and in consequence many more outsiders who wanted a safe seat.

How did Cornwall come to have 44 MPs?

In the Middle Ages Cornwall had a perfectly reasonable representation in Parliament. Several substantial boroughs each had two MPs, Bodmin, Helston, Launceston, Liskeard, Penryn, Truro and Lostwithiel, the last having been a more significant town than it subsequently became. There were also two 'knights of the shire'.

A dramatic change occurred during the reigns of Mary (1553-58) and Elizabeth (1558-1603) when further boroughs were enfranchised, each with two MPs. Most of them were too small to justify representation.

It was a clear case of gerrymandering by the governments of those queens, intended to provide reliable votes in the Commons. Under the Tudors, and even more under the Stuarts, there was increasing resistance in the Commons to the levels of taxation demanded by the monarchy, so the governments needed to fight back.

Why the emphasis on Cornwall? The answer was the Duchy. The Duchy was founded by Edward III in 1337 as a source of income for his eldest son, Edward 'the Black Prince'. Whilst it did not possess all land in the county, the Duchy was powerful even in areas it did not own, with stannary rights over tin production and ownership of the coasts and rivers. It would have been against the interest of almost any Cornishman to incur the antagonism of the Duchy.

Succession to the Duchy is unlike most other titles; it is reserved for the monarch's eldest son, the heir to the throne. If he dies before the monarch, it does not pass to a descendant but to his eldest surviving brother. If there is no eligible son, the Duchy goes into abeyance and its revenues revert to the monarch. Neither Queen Mary or Queen Elizabeth had sons. Their governments reckoned that they could hold Cornish borough 'patrons' in thrall, and would also be reimbursed by the patrons for creating the boroughs.

The issue was certainly noticed in political discussions over the centuries. John Evelyn, in his diary for 22 May 1685, when the first parliament under the Catholic James II was convened and many were worried that the Church of England would suffer in consequence, reported:

> Mr [Edward] Seymour made a bold speech against many elections, and would have had those members who (he claimed) were obnoxious [i.e. subject to legal challenge] to withdraw, till they had cleared the matter of their being legally returned; but no one seconded him. The truth is, there were many of the new members whose elections and returns were universally censured, many of them being persons of no condition, or interest, in the nation, or places for which they served, especially in Devon, Cornwall, Norfolk, etc, said to have been recommended by the Court, and from the effect of the new charters changing the electors. It was reported that Lord Bath carried down with him

into Cornwall no fewer than fifteen charters, so that some called him the Prince Elector....

The new charters allowed the monarch to ban candidates they didn't like.

Some extremes

The rottenest borough of all was Bossiney, which included Tintagel, with just 308 inhabitants in 1831. In the Tudor period alone, Bossiney's MPs included Sir Francis Walsingham (Queen Elizabeth's spymaster), Sir Francis Bacon (a statesman who is also regarded as the founder of the scientific method) and Sir Francis Drake.

Bossiney's two patrons, the Earl of Mount Edgcumbe and the Wortley family, usually agreed to nominate one MP each, and they bribed the voters with well paid positions in the Padstow customs house. (Needless to say, this did not help the prevention of smuggling!) An Act of Parliament of 1782 attempted to stop such abuses and customs officers and other government officials were banned from voting. In the 1784 election Bossiney had just nine eligible voters, but eight of them still had posts in the customs house. The two MPs for Bossiney were therefore elected by a single voter – the vicar of Tintagel.

And then there were none. One of the finest reports of corruption comes from Bere Alston, just across the Tamar from Calstock, enfranchised in 1584 in the same flurry of creations as the Cornish rotten boroughs. In 1830 *The Times* carried the following report:

> Dr Butler [the Portreeve, who was Returning Officer for the borough] ... met the voters under a great tree, the place usually chosen for the purpose of election. During the time the Portreeve was reading the acts of Parliament usually read on such occasions, one of the voters handed in to him a card containing the names of two candidates, proposed by himself and seconded by his friend. He was told this was too early. Before the reading was completed, the voter on the other side handed in a card corresponding with the former, which he was told was too late. The meeting broke up. The Portreeve and assistants adjourned to a public house in the neighbourhood, and then and there made a

return of Lord Lovaine and Mr Blackett, which was not signed by a single person having a vote.

The 20 year old Lord Lovaine (1810-1899) later became the 6th Earl of Northumberland and was a cabinet minister in Disraeli's governments. Christopher Blackett was the son of a Northumberland coal owner. Is it surprising that the locals were unimpressed?

In the 1818 election Grampound returned two members but a petition was launched claiming gross bribery, not for the first time there, and a Bill was introduced to disenfranchise the borough. This would have passed, except that the proposed new parliamentary constituency to replace Grampound was Leeds. Shock, horror! Leeds was far too industrial and would elect radical non-conformists. Instead an amendment suggested that the two replacement MPs should be for Yorkshire as a whole, and that passed.

After 1832

By the 1832 Act, Cornwall was reduced from 42 MPs to 14 – the most brutal cut faced by any county but undoubtedly needed. The whole system of voter registration was changed: more men were added to the lists, meaning 15% of Cornish men had the vote instead of 9% – but the average across England and Wales rose to 22.5%.

The secret ballot was not introduced until 1872, so landlords and employers continued to send observers to watch the voters. Boisterous nomination sessions, lavish servings of food and drink, and occasional bribery, persisted for decades. Until 1918 only 40% of men had the vote, and not till 1928 did all British adults have the vote.

The Cornish rotten boroughs with their date of creation

Newport   1529

West Looe   1535

Grampound   1547

Mitchell   1547

Saltash   1552

Bossiney   1553

Camelford   1553

St Ives   1558

Tregony   1559

St Germans   1562

St Mawes   1562

East Looe   1571

Fowey   1571

Callington   1585

Some MPs who were elected for Cornish boroughs

Of course it was not the MPs who were rotten (not all of them, anyway) but the system. The individuals selected here are a small sample, chosen in part because they are famous or interesting, and are limited to the period between 1553 and 1832. After 1832 there were no rotten MPs, though some were still reportedly useless. Some of those chosen could in fact be proud of their parliamentary activity – for example fighting back against the absolutism of the Stuarts – while others scarcely bothered to attend.

Sir Francis Walsingham   c.1532-1590

Queen Elizabeth's 'Spymaster' was a lawyer's son, born in Kent. The family were very well connected. He too became a lawyer, exiled himself during Catholic Mary's reign, and on her death returned to England. With the help of the Earl of Bedford he was elected MP for Bossiney in 1559, but at the next election opted for Lyme Regis and subsequently as a county MP for Surrey.

Very soon he became part of Queen Elizabeth's governing group, and worked with William Cecil to break the Ridolfi plot, which had hoped to replace the Queen with the Catholic Mary Queen of Scots. He was appointed ambassador to France, and later Secretary of State to the Queen. He encouraged exploratory voyages, including Drake's circumnavigation, mercantile trading and exploration of America. He played a major part in the complicated diplomacy of the period, including negotiating the Treaty of Berwick with James VI of Scotland.

During his time in France he had seen the horrors of the St Bartholomew's Day massacre, in which thousands of leading Huguenots were slaughtered, and his fears of a similar event occurring in England made him willing to use any means possible to prevent it, including torture. He used informers, intercepted letters in order to find Catholic priests and likely conspirators, and employed spies within the French embassy, as well as inventing other espionage techniques. One plot to invade England was thwarted. Then he trapped Mary Queen of Scots (already in captivity in England) into endorsing a plot to kill Elizabeth, and had Mary tried and found guilty.

When Elizabeth kept hesitating to sign the death warrant, Walsingham suggested to Mary's custodian that the Queen wished him to 'shorten her life'. In the end Mary was executed, with Elizabeth rather unconvincingly claiming she had not meant this to happen.

Walsingham developed an extraordinary spy network right across Europe, and was made aware of the Armada invasion threat two years before 1588, which enabled England to take active steps to defend itself. After his death, to Protestants he was a hero who had prevented a violent Catholic takeover, to Catholics a ruthless and intolerant villain. Perhaps both were right?

Sir Richard Grenville   1542-1591

In my childhood, when the world map in school atlases was disproportionately pink, Sir Richard was one of those heroes who were rolled out to inspire children to become the next imperial generation. Tennyson's ballad 'The Revenge', with its first line 'At Flores in the Azores Sir Richard Grenville lay,' was very popular.

But a contemporary described him as 'a man of intolerable pride and insatiable ambition'. The Grenvilles of Stowe near Kilkhampton were a gentry family with a military tradition. Sir Richard's grandfather had been Knight Marshal of Calais; his father was master of the *Mary Rose* and drowned when it capsized. They were probably the second richest family in Cornwall. Richard inherited at the age of nine. He was at various times a knight of the shire and High Sheriff of Cornwall.

He spent some time at the Inns of Court, which were the normal finishing school for gentlemen. In 1562 he killed a man in a street brawl – gangs of sword-toting young bloods were a feature of London life – but he was soon pardoned. He spent some time learning the soldier's trade in Hungary, then in 1568 was involved in a failed colonial settlement in Cork, but had to withdraw. His possessions were extensive both in Cornwall and Devon, including Buckland Abbey, which he rebuilt in its present form, and the whole town of Bideford which he set about developing with a new quay and a town charter, giving up some of his manorial privileges but creating a bustling and profitable port.

He was financially interested in various privateering ventures, as well as a proposal for a voyage to discover the supposed North-West Passage from the Pacific side – but this was probably just an excuse for piracy. The Queen vetoed it for political reasons.

In the event it was Francis Drake (seen by Grenville as a low-born upstart) who made his fame and fortune from a round-the-world voyage, and on his return eclipsed Grenville as the leading man in the Plymouth area. Seething quietly, Grenville put Buckfast Abbey up for sale, only to find that Drake immediately snapped it up. Grenville's general policy was to sell his remoter estates, and consolidate around Kilkhampton and Bideford.

In 1585 he made what seems to have been his first major voyage, to plant a settlement in Virginia, for which Sir Walter Raleigh held the charter. Again, the main intention seems to have been to establish a privateering base rather than a colony, but the settlers failed to find a suitable deep water anchorage. Grenville took some lucrative prizes on his way back. Returning the following year with supplies, he found the base deserted. That man Drake had collected the unhappy settlers a few weeks previously. This time on the way back Grenville sacked towns in the Azores.

By now war with Spain was becoming serious and Grenville was instructed to stay in England and lend his ships to Drake as part of the defence against the Armada. Drake later took the *Revenge* for his attack on Lisbon. That expedition was disastrous: Drake was now sidelined (one can imagine Grenville's glee) and a new policy instituted. An English fleet would hover in the Atlantic to intercept the Spanish treasure fleets.

Consequently, in 1591 Sir Richard Grenville, under the command of Lord Thomas Howard, lay indeed at Flores in the Azores refitting his ship. The Spanish, however, knew what the English were up to and sent a vastly larger fleet (tradition says 53 ships) to pounce on them. Admiral Howard was warned, and he ordered a tactical withdrawal. All the other English ships got away, but Grenville seems to have deliberately delayed, then chose to sail into the middle of the Spanish fleet, where a galleon three times the tonnage of the *Revenge* grappled her and tried to board. An epic battle followed.

The fight continued through the night and by dawn the *Revenge* was a dismasted wreck surrounded by Spanish ships, two of which later sank. Honourable terms were offered, but Grenville (knowing himself fatally wounded) wanted to blow up or sink his ship. He was prevented by the officers. He was given the best care possible by the Spanish, who recorded his last words, which consisted of pride in his own achievement and scorn for the men who had chosen not to die – but the scorn was omitted from the English translation.

Tennyson's poem gave a rose-coloured view of the final action. Modern interpretations suggest Sir Richard had deliberately disobeyed an order and sacrificed one of England's best ships and its crew, and the objectives of Lord Howard's mission, all for personal glory or in a fit of battle madness.

Thomas Cromwell   c.1540-c.1611

No, not Hilary Mantel's Thomas Cromwell!

In fact he was that Thomas's grandson, and was probably born the same year that Henry VIII executed his facilitator, who had been MP for Taunton. Thomas Cromwell junior was MP for Fowey (1571), Bodmin (1572-81), Preston, Lancashire (1584-5), and Grampound (1586-7 and 1589). He took his job as an MP very seriously, keeping diaries of parliamentary proceedings, and became an acknowledged authority, much valued on parliamentary committees. A bit boring perhaps, but very helpful to the Speaker and to modern historians of parliament.

The reason he has been included here is that, whilst a good MP, he typifies the rotten borough problem. His parents were Gregory, first Baron Cromwell and Elizabeth Seymour, sister of Henry VIII's third wife, Jane Seymour, who died giving birth to the future Edward VI. His father's connections at Court included Sir William Cecil, who probably helped him to his Cornish seats, and Sir Ralph Sadler, Chancellor of the Duchy of Lancaster.

Coming from this very privileged family, he first became an MP at the age of 21. When he retired from parliament he went to live near King's Lynn, Norfolk. He appears to have had no connection at all with Cornwall.

Sir Francis Bacon, Viscount St Albans 1561-1626

His father was Lord Keeper of the Great Seal; his uncle William Cecil, Lord Burghley, was Queen Elizabeth's chief adviser for most of her reign. To that privileged start in life he added great intelligence, and became both a philosopher and a statesman, declaring that he had three goals, to uncover truth, to serve his country and to serve his church. His philosophy was much more successful than his political career, of which more later.

Later in the 17th century and throughout the 18th Bacon was regarded as the father of the scientific method, and he was much admired in France and America as well as in Britain for both his scientific and political thinking.

In science he said it was vital to collect painstakingly all the evidence for a question, look at it objectively, see if this leads to a hypothesis ('induction'), then test the hypothesis by experiment. It was important that this should not be done secretly but in consort with other people; creative and cooperative dispute was recommended – an idea which led via a Gresham College group to the founding of the hugely important Royal Society.

It was also vital to be aware of the 'idols of the mind' – the pre-judgements about how things work that exist in all our minds, collectively and individually – and to eliminate them when assessing the evidence. He wrote: 'If a man will begin with certainties, he shall end in doubts, but if he will be content to begin with doubts, he shall end in certainties.' (He was himself not immune from idols of the mind, believing in a providential God and that 'all knowledge is to be limited by religion'.)

His approach to politics was deliberately similar, i.e. based on data and objectivity. The first necessity was written histories, concentrating on facts rather than trying to prove an existing theory as to cause and effect, and without trying to entertain the reader. When sufficient histories are available, then it is possible, as with science, to hypothesise. Practical policies can then be created which have a strong chance of succeeding. The ethics of those policies can be disregarded if they are for the long-term benefit of your society. This is very similar to the advice of his Italian predecessor Machiavelli, though without the extremes of 'Machiavellianism'.

Now for his career: after a standard education at Cambridge and Grays Inn, he accompanied the English ambassador to France on a tour to several French cities, and to Italy and Spain, studying languages and civil law in each country as well as being engaged in basic diplomatic tasks. His father died in 1579, when he was 18, and he returned to London looking for advancement.

He was elected MP for Bossiney in 1581, Melcombe in Dorset in 1584, Taunton 1586, Liverpool 1588, Middlesex 1593, three times for Ipswich and finally Cambridge University in 1614, before entering the House of Lords. His uncle helped him progress rapidly at the bar, but he was disappointed not to be appointed to financially rewarding posts, and the Queen seems to have snubbed him as potential Attorney General or Solicitor General, preferring his rival Edward Coke, but he did become the first QC – Queen's Counsel.

Things got better under James VI and I. He was knighted in 1603, created Baron Verulam in 1618 and Viscount St Albans in 1621. In the Commons he supported the King's 'arbitrary policies' and extravagant spending, which doubtless helped him become first Solicitor General, then Attorney General, then in 1618 Lord Chancellor.

He was strongly in favour of a full union of England and Scotland and also of bringing in Ireland and the Netherlands. (By coincidence, it was another MP for Bossiney, Simon Harcourt, who was comissioner for arranging the Union with Scotland in 1707.) Bacon was also influential in establishing British colonies in Virginia, Carolina and Newfoundland.

Despite the lucrative posts he now held, Bacon was falling into debt, and at the same time acquiring a body of enemies in Parliament. In 1621 a parliamentary committee charged him with corruption. To everyone's astonishment he fully confessed to taking bribes as a judge, was fined £40,000 and committed to the Tower. It has been suggested that his confession was the result of blackmail for being gay: he had married, but only when 46, and to a bride aged 13. The King released him, and Bacon spent his last five years writing voluminously.

Sir Francis Drake   c.1540-1596

Drake was born at Crowndale Farm, a mile down the River Tavy from Tavistock. His uncle was the main tenant, and his father Edward was a shearman in the cloth industry. The family was well respected, and Francis Drake's godfather was Francis Russell, the future Earl of Bedford.

The exact year of his birth is unknown, but he was still a child when the family moved to Gillingham in Kent – in fear of the Prayer Book Rebellion and its Catholic mobs, or so Drake himself believed. But in fact his father had in 1548 been indicted for two highway robberies, for which he was pardoned that December, by which time he had already left Tavistock; the Rebellion was not till the next year. The details are unknown. Was it really highway robbery or unsophisticated debt collection? Why was he pardoned? Given Francis' own later pre-dilection for seaway robbery in a righteous (maybe) cause, it would be nice to know!

The family lived in a boat, probably a hulk beached beside the Medway, and Edward Drake made a small living informally reading prayers and preaching to naval sailors: he was made Vicar of Upchurch in 1566. Francis himself became a very zealous and uncompromising Puritan. He learned his trade as apprentice to the skipper of a small coasting vessel; when the man died without heirs, he left his boat to Drake, who sold it and returned to Plymouth, seeking employment from his relatives the Hawkins brothers, a wealthy merchant family newly involved in the slave trade.

There is no room here for full details of his life, but he became internationally famous in his own day, a great hero to Protestant Europe and the devil incarnate to Catholics. There are several biographies, including a brief one by Alex White published by Bossiney, and both his adventures and complex character make for a good read.

As a result of his early experiences with John Hawkins in the Caribbean, where he felt he had been betrayed by the Spanish viceroy who controlled it, he began a lifetime of revenge against the King of Spain. His vengeance brought him both wealth and prestige.

The total amount he brought back in 1580 from his three year circumnavigation is unknown, but it was probably at least £400,000, at a time when the Queen's annual revenue was around £250,000. The Queen, as a major investor in the circumnavigation voyage, was delighted both by the cash and by the humiliation of Spain.

He seems to have been elected as an MP in a by-election in 1581, possibly for Camelford, but it was at the tail end of a parliament and he was excused attendance. At the next election in 1584 he was elected for Bossiney, unanimously by all nine voters, all loyal to the Earl of Bedford, Drake's godfather. He was appointed to several committees for which he had relevant knowledge – fisheries, Raleigh's American colony, the Navy, Plymouth harbour, the Devon cloth trade – and also one on which he was passionate, for the better observation of the Sabbath: that resulted in a Bill which was passed, but the Queen refused to sign it as it was too strict: it even included a ban on hunting, which was a favourite pastime of hers.

Drake missed the next two parliaments, being too busy singeing the King of Spain's beard, playing bowls before chasing the Armada, etc, but in 1593 he was returned for Plymouth, and at the same time was Deputy Lord Lieutenant for Devon. In parliament he took an active part in securing a 'subsidy' (a one-off tax for national defence) and chaired a committee for 'better preserving the navy of this realm'. Other matters of interest were salted fish, recusancy, poor relief and aid for injured soldiers and sailors. So he appears to have been an active MP with concern both for the navy and for Plymouth, if not for Bossiney.

He was also very active within Plymouth's local government, and procured an Act for a leat taking fresh water from the River Meavy to Mill Bay in Plymouth. (He took personal advantage of this to set up six mills of his own which he could lease!)

He died of a fever in Portobelo Bay, Panama in January 1596, leaving no children and a will which by its nature caused decades of litigation between various branches of the Drake family.

Richard Carew 1555-1620

Richard Carew of Antony (a characteristically Cornish way of distinguishing himself from the numerous other West Country branches of that family) was born in 1555, just nine years before Shakespeare. He was educated at Oxford, becoming a 'gentleman-commoner' at the age of 11. In Elizabethan days the gentry used Oxbridge more like a school than a university and, as was then normal, Carew moved on at the age of 19 to one of the London Inns of Court (the Middle Temple) for his higher education.

Carew's studious habits at Oxford and the Middle Temple brought him into contact with the leading lights of both the literary and antiquarian worlds. He wrote poetry, which in those days was mainly circulated in manuscript between like-minded people. By this means Carew knew of and admired Shakespeare as a poet; probably he never saw a Shakespeare play – and they did not move in the same social circles.

Carew was also part of a group which began to meet at the house of Sir Robert Cotton, and included William Camden (another Oxford contemporary) and John Stow. This group became the Society of Antiquaries, and was a key element in the development of historical studies in England .

But Richard Carew's interests extended beyond libraries. As a member of the Cornish gentry he was pleased to take a full part in the county administration, which at that time was almost entirely devolved from the Queen to the gentry. Carew fulfilled such roles as Sheriff of the county, MP for Saltash (1584) and in 1586 became a Deputy Lieutenant of the county with 500 men under his command. He was responsible for the defence of the Cawsand area at the time of the Armada, for which he cannot be envied. Sir Walter Raleigh had been made Lieutenant.

Carew's great *Survey of Cornwall* was originally written for circulation among the gentry. Its numerous family genealogies were doubtless of interest to the marriage arrangers among them. Carew also has many of the social and very English prejudices of his class; for example, he writes patronisingly of Cornish tinners:

If you did see how aptly they cast the ground for conveying the water, by compassings and turnings to shun such hills and valleys as [hinder] them by their too much height or lowness, you would wonder how so great skill could couch in so base a cabin as their (otherwise) thickclouded brains.

The great achievement of the *Survey of Cornwall*, especially compared with topographical works from the following three centuries, is that Carew writes to a large extent from personal observation, rather than reworking earlier authors' materials, and he has decided for himself what he thinks is worth noting. He had travelled about the county on his administrative duties, seen for himself what was happening and been able to get detailed information from his colleagues, for example on mining techniques from Sir Francis Godolphin.

Sir Walter Raleigh c.1552-1618

Raleigh (it could also be spelt in ten other ways!) was born at Hayes Barton in East Devon (the house survives), the fifth son in a Protestant gentry family. Sir Humphrey Gilbert was his half-brother, Sir Richard Grenville his cousin. As a fifth son he had little chance of inheriting land, and volunteered as a soldier first with the Huguenots in France, then in the suppression of a rebellion in Ireland, during which, after the siege of Smerwick, he and another officer executed 600 soldiers who had surrendered. Accused of this much later, Raleigh explained that he was just obeying orders. He also made two voyages with Sir Humphrey Gilbert.

Raleigh had multiple connections at Court: his aunt had been the Queen's governess. When he was introduced at Court the Queen seems to have been bowled over by this handsome soldier and before long he received a number of profitable appointments and grants of land – including 40,000 acres in Ireland. In 1585 he was made Warden of the Stannaries, Steward of the Duchy and Lord Lieutenant of Cornwall, which meant he was in charge of the defence of Cornwall at the time of the Armada – but since he was given no troops other than the local militias, it is fortunate the Spanish didn't land.

Sir Humphrey Gilbert and Raleigh received a royal charter to explore and colonise land overseas 'not actually possessed by any

Christian Prince'. This resulted in the first English attempt at colonisation, on the island of Roanoke, though it was more a privateering base than a colony. The attempt failed. Raleigh also organised a number of privateering expeditions.

He was appointed captain of the Queen's guard, a very influential position since he could control access to the Queen (and in consequence take backhanders). In 1591 he married Bess Throckmorton, one of the Queen's ladies in waiting, but without the Queen's knowledge, which was forbidden: Elizabeth was understandably concerned that there were always plots against her life, and she wanted to know what were the family connections of those immediately around her. When she found out about the marriage, Raleigh and his wife were sent to the Tower. In 1592 he was released, since one of his fleets had captured an incredibly valuable prize: he kindly donated £80,000 to the Queen.

He had heard stories of gold-rich 'El Dorado' in what is now Venezuela, and made an expedition there in 1595: his account of the voyage somewhat overstated his discoveries.

Raleigh was MP for Devon in 1584 and 1586, in 1593 for Mitchell, in 1597 for Dorset and in 1601 for Cornwall. During the 1590s he took a very active part in the Commons and was vocal on the need to grant the Queen 'subsidies' to defend against Spain. Nevertheless, it was a long time before he got back into the Queen's favour, and then she died. He hoped for better things when James became king, but his rivals beat him to it and briefed the new king against him. James remarked 'Oh my soul, mon, I have heard rawly of thee.' In fact he was accused (improbably) of treason, found guilty and put once again in the Tower, where he remained for 13 years, writing his *Historie of the World*.

Then James released him – though still under sentence of death – so that he could find El Dorado and enrich James. But James made clear Raleigh absolutely had to avoid conflict with Spain, with which there was an uneasy peace.

Unfortunately one of Raleigh's commanders, together with his own son Walter, disobeyed their orders and made a rash attack on a Spanish outpost. To placate the Spanish, Raleigh was beheaded.

Sir John Eliot   1592-1632

John Eliot was born on his father's estate at St Germans, and educated at Blundell's School, Exeter College, Oxford, and then the Inns of Court. By the age of 22 he was an MP for St Germans and a friend of George Villiers, the future Duke of Buckingham, through whose patronage he was knighted. In 1619 he became Vice-Admiral of Devon and trapped a notorious pirate. This, in corrupt Stuart England, was a serious mistake since the pirate had a protector at court: Eliot spent nearly four months in the Marshalsea prison for having caught the villain.

For the time being he remained a friend and supporter of Buckingham, but he made powerful speeches in Parliament demanding that its ancient privileges and liberties should be respected. In the Parliament of 1626 he found himself leader of the House, opposing the incompetent Buckingham and in effect King Charles himself. It was Eliot who carried Buckingham's impeachment to the Lords, comparing him to Sejanus. For this he was sent to the Tower, but the Commons effectively went on strike. The king dissolved Parliament and released Eliot, though depriving him of the Vice-Admiralty.

In 1627 Eliot was again imprisoned, this time for refusing on principle to pay forced loans. At the subsequent election in 1628 he stood for a county seat instead of a rotten borough and (to the horror of the Cornish gentry) appealed directly to non-gentry voters and was elected. He was now at the forefront of democratic opposition to the king. The speaker was forcibly held in his chair while Eliot's resolutions against taxation (and also against both Roman Catholics and Arminians, because he believed 'we may be in danger to have our whole Religion overthrown') were read to the House. Along with seven other MPs, he was arrested and sent to the Marshalsea, then charged with 'conspiracy to resist the King's order', fined £2000 and sent to the Tower.

Charles I by this time hated Eliot and ensured that his treatment in the Tower over the next four years was harsh. When he died, probably of tuberculosis but at the time some suspected poison, the petty and vindictive king refused to release his body and it was buried in St Peter ad Vincula, the chapel within the Tower.

Eliot was by no means a rotten MP. He represented his own people and fought against the dangerously autocratic ambitions of the Stuarts.

Edward Hyde, Earl of Clarendon 1609-1674

Hyde's father and grandfather had both been MPs, and he was elected to the Long Parliament for Saltash in 1640. He was always a centrist, and he felt Charles I's attempt to rule without Parliament had been wrong; he voted for Strafford's attainder and attacked prerogative courts and the Laudian bishops. But as the dispute grew fiercer he moved further towards the royalist side, and when war broke out, went to join the King, as his main political adviser.

In 1644 the 14-year-old Prince of Wales was put nominally in charge of military affairs in the South-West, and Hyde was appointed to his Council of Advisers. Once the royal cause was clearly lost, two years later, Hyde went with Prince Charles to Jersey, entrusted by the King as his mentor. But he would not accompany Charles when his father told him to join the Queen his mother in France, because he feared Charles would turn Catholic.

Hyde was always in favour of moderation. After the King's execution, he dissuaded Charles from involving the French, Spanish or Dutch. An invading foreign army would not bring longterm peace. He was also very much a Church of England supporter, and always opposed involving Catholics or Presbyterians. He described Charles' negotiations with the Presbyterian Scots as 'folly and atheism'. The disaster of the Battle of Worcester certainly proved the folly.

Charles was then persuaded to wait for the mood in England to change, which in time it did. Clarendon as Lord Chancellor composed the Declaration of Breda, in which Charles promised amnesty for all who surrendered within 40 days, and a degree of religious tolerance (details to be decided by Parliament) if Charles returned as king. In 1660 Charles was indeed restored to the throne, amid great rejoicing in England, but the religious tolerance Hyde had sought failed to appear.

Hyde was created Earl of Clarendon at the Coronation; he was famously eloquent and self-confident – but that could create enemies at Court. There were hot-headed and politically inexperienced courtiers who thought it was time for a change. Clarendon openly despised the King's mistress, Lady Castlemaine, and she worked against him.

The Duke of York, the future James II, had unfortunately seduced Hyde's daughter and then married her, much to Hyde's displeasure since James was a Catholic. But with Charles failing to produce a legitimate heir, it was widely assumed that Hyde had plotted the marriage so that his daughter would become the next queen. (She didn't, but two of her daughters did become queens, as Mary II and then Anne.)

Worst of all, Clarendon lacked tact, and was still treating Charles, in his mid-thirties, as though he was a teenager. His enemies in Court and in Parliament joined together and made Clarendon, with no justification, the scapegoat for the disastrous loss of the Second Dutch War. He was charged with high treason in 1667. Rather than have him tried, Charles sent him into exile, glad to see the back of him. Clarendon spent the remainder of his life on the Continent, writing his great work *The History of the Rebellion*.

William Prynne   1600-1669

One of the most contentious characters of his highly factious times, Prynne was born near Bath, educated at Oriel College, Oxford, and became a lawyer. He was also a prolific writer, promoting Puritan views. To drink toasts or celebrate Christmas was sinful. Men wearing their hair long was 'unseemly and unlawful unto Christians', whilst for women to cut their hair short was 'mannish, unnatural, impudent and unchristian'. Barberous views, some might say.

He published *Histriomastix*, 'the actor's scourge', a book attacking the theatre in general and women's roles on stage in particular. By chance, at around the same time that it was published in 1633 (though after it was written) the Queen and her ladies-in-waiting took part in a play performed at court. The book was taken to be an attack on the King and Queen; it was condemned to be 'burnt, in the most public manner that can be'; Prynne was tried, sentenced to life imprisonment, fined £5000 (at a time when an agricultural labourer might earn £25 in a year), expelled from Lincoln's Inn so that he could no longer practice as a lawyer, and put in the pillory both at Westminster and at Cheapside, where his ears were cut off and the book was burned in front of him, so that he was nearly smothered by the smoke.

While in the Tower he wrote more pamphlets, resulting in a further fine, branding on the cheek with 'SL' (seditious libeller, or as he insisted *stigmata laudis*, mark of praise) and to have the stumps of his ears removed.

He was released by the Long Parliament in 1640 and restored to the bar. On his return to London there were great celebrations, with a hundred coaches and thousands of people forming a procession.

By 1643 Prynne was publising pamphlets in favour of deposing Charles for having started the Civil War and in his *The Soveraigne Power of Parliaments and Kingdoms* he had already justified tyrannicide. He wanted the state, rather than the church, to impose a binding ecclesiastical discipline and to clamp down on heresies and schisms. (One suspects that he would never have agreed with any definition of a heresy unless he'd defined it himself.) By 1645, whilst not in Parliament, he was involved in politics, holding offices and organising the biassed trial of Archbishop Laud, predictably condemning him to death.

The Parliamentary side in the Civil Wars was far from united, with some concentrating on politics and others more concerned with religion. Within the relgious faction, there was a serious division between Presbyterians, who wanted a uniform religious discipline to hold the state together, and the Independents such as John Lilburne, who said that persecution of individual consciences was the work of the devil. Prynne was a strong Presbyterian, who persecuted Lilburne.

The New Model Army, and Cromwell, were increasingly seen as Independents and therefore dangerous, though that was probably an exaggeration: they were more moderate than their opponents. Prynne wrote vehemently against the Army.

Once the King had been defeated militarily, there were endless attempts to reach an agreement with him, but Charles was not a man to be trusted, even escaping and starting a second civil war, which was fortunately short-lived. Prynne had wanted Parliament to accept the King's word and do a deal. When Charles was finally put on trial, it is doubtful that many people wanted him executed, but his refusal to acknowledge the court made that all but inevitable.

Prynne was 'elected' to Parliament for Newport (the northern suburb of Launceston) in November 1648, and immediately spoke out against the Army. Two days later, in 'Pride's Purge', the Army entered Parliament, arresting many members including Prynne, and expelling others, leaving 'the Rump' which they could rely on.

The arrested members were soon released, and Prynne retired to his home near Bath, where he wrote against Cromwell's regime, opposed allowing Jews back into England as Cromwell proposed, refused to pay taxes to an illegitimate government, and was imprisoned for three years. After Cromwell's death he tried to re-enter the Rump Parliament, but was for the most part prevented by armed guards, until the arrival of General Monck in 1660. Prynne then played a significant role in the Restoration.

He was subsequently elected for Bath, but was not a major figure in Parliament, where his continued non-conformity was unwelcome. Charles II rewarded him with several public offices, including Keeper of the Records at the Tower, kindly shutting his eyes to Prynne's presbyterianism.

Thomas Povey   1615-1702

Thomas Povey was a London merchant with a strong interest (not least for his own financial benefit) in politics. During the Commonwealth he was MP for Liskeard in 1646 and for Bossiney in 1659.

He acquired a number of posts, first under Oliver Cromwell then under Charles II – so many that he was never able to cover them all effectively, and exasperated his colleagues, notably Samuel Pepys, by his incompetence. He makes many appearances in Pepys' diary.

Among other posts, he was Treasurer to the Duke of York, Receiver General of the Committee for Foreign Plantations, and Treasurer to the Commission for Tangier. Povey's brothers held posts in Jamaica and Barbados and a cousin was Lieutenant Governor of Massachusetts.

He was a member of the Royal Society, skilled in mechanics and admired for his good taste in domestic architecture and collecting paintings.

Davies Giddy, later Davies Gilbert 1767-1839

Son of a curate at St Erth, he was educated at a mathematical academy and graduated from Pembroke College, Oxford, having studied science and mathematics. Whilst he seems to have achieved little himself, he was able to help Richard Trevithick, Jonathan Hornblower, Thomas Telford and above all Humphry Davy. He was involved in scientific societies both in Cornwall and London, becoming President of the Royal Society – though his indecisiveness in that role seems to have caused problems.

He accepted a nomination as MP for Helston in 1804. A contemporary who met him shortly afterwards on a coach reported:

> His conversation was the most entertaining and full of information, his appearance disgustingly mean. Since that time one who knows him intimately has told me that his coming into Parliament was equally extraordinary with everything else about him— inasmuch that with decided opposition principles and an independent fortune [actually not the case at that time] he had accepted Sir Christopher Hawkins's offer of being brought in professedly to support the [prime] minister for the time being, whoever he may be, in order to foster Sir Christopher's jobs, and that he makes no secret of the wish he entertains in contradiction to every vote he gives.

At the 1806 election, to Giddy's annoyance, his patron found someone who would pay him for the Helston seat and required that he vacate it; Giddy obtained a Bodmin seat instead. At that stage of his career he was hoping for a place, but later was able to avoid accepting anything arduous. In 1808 he managed to marry Mary Anne Gilbert of Eastbourne, heir to £100,000, changing his name to Gilbert in 1817 so that he could inherit her uncle's estates, after which he was free to behave as he pleased.

He was a regular attender at the House, and spoke frequently, consistently promoting Cornish interests – voting against the salt tax because it hurt the pilchard industry, and against a public house bill which would have allowed publicans to dispense with pewter mugs. He claimed that Humphrey Davy had discovered a 'galvanic influence', by which beer tasted better when drunk out of pewter (which is largely composed of tin). Another member said he hoped science would soon discover that roast beef should be eaten off pewter plates, as that too would help the Cornish tin mines.

He seems to have been reactionary in his political views, believing that democracy was the route to despotism, and that the landed and mercantile interests should control Parliament. He voted against Catholic emancipation, and against the removal of the death penalty for theft. He also opposed universal education:

> However specious in theory the project might be of giving education to the labouring classes of the poor, it would, in effect, be found to be prejudicial to their morals and happiness; it would teach them to despise their lot in life, instead of making them good servants in agriculture and other laborious employments to which their rank in society had destined them; instead of teaching them the virtue of subordination, it would render them factious and refractory, as is evident in the manufacturing counties; it would enable them to read seditious pamphlets, vicious books and publications against Christianity; it would render them insolent to their superiors.

After the 1832 Reform Act, he left Parliament.

Edward Gibbon   1737-1794

Gibbon was the author of a major historical work, *The Decline and Fall of the Roman Empire* in six-volumes. He was also a typically useless eighteenth century back-bencher. His *Memoirs*, which he insisted should not be published in his lifetime, give some helpful insights into the election system of his time. Apart from one weekend visit, it is doubtful if he ever came to Cornwall. As he once joked, 'Why is a fat man like a Cornish borough? Because he never sees his member.'

He was the eldest of seven children, but all six of his siblings died in infancy, and his mother died giving birth to the last of them. Neither parent cared much for him, nor he for them. He had a physical disability as a child, with frequent illnesses which disrupted his schooling – possibly to his advantage, since he read extensively and enthusiastically what he himself had chosen.

His grandfather had been a successful merchant, but was stripped of 90% of his assets by the government for his part in the massively damaging 'South Sea Bubble', as a director of the South Sea Company. But he soon became rich again. (Had he concealed his assets?) Gibbon's father, also Edward Gibbon, preferred the life of an extravagant gentleman at Buriton near Petersfield, Hants, and lost most of his wealth, obliging Gibbon to sign away the entail on the estate in return for an annuity of £300. His father was a Tory MP for Southampton, and Gibbon described the election:

> The Whig candidates had a majority of the resident voters; but the corporation was firm in the Tory interest. A sudden creation of 170 [actually 117] new freemen turned the scale. and a supply was readily obtained of respectable volunteers who flocked from all parts of England to support their political friends.

Gibbon was sent to Magdalen College, Oxford aged 15, where the teaching was non-existent. He read a lot, absorbed Catholic ideas, and converted to Catholicism. His father was appalled, removed him from Oxford and sent him to Protestant Lausanne – a city which he soon came to love, and where he returned to the Church of England. After five years, he was recalled on his 21st birthday so that he could sign away the entail.

He then spent four years full-time as a captain in the South Hampshire militia; there was a war with France at the time, but he never saw military action. His father wanted him to be an MP but Gibbon managed to avoid it: he thought himself unsuitable.

He then spent two and a half years on a Grand Tour in France and Italy, and on his return was promoted to Lieutenant-Colonel Commander of the militia, but he didn't enjoy it and resigned in 1770.

> It is a melancholy truth that my father's death, not unhappy for himself, was the only event that could save me from a hopeless life of obscurity and indigence.

His father died in 1770, though for a time there were still financial problems and he had to sell property to clear a mortgage. He sent his affectionate stepmother packing, to Bath, against her wishes, and himself moved to London.

I had now attained the solid comforts of life, a convenient well furnished house, a domestic table, half a dozen chosen servants, my own carriage, and all those decent luxuries whose value is more sensibly felt the longer they are enjoyed.

By the friendship of Mr (now Lord) Eliot [of Port Eliot], who had married my first cousin, I was returned at the [1774] election for the borough of Liskeard… After a fleeting, elusive hope, prudence condemned me to acquiescence in the humble state of a mute.

The arrangements were not quite as simple as might be imagined. Eliot had six seats at his disposal.

After some idle conversation he told me, that if I was desirous of being in Parliament, he had an *independent* seat very much at my service. You may suppose my answer, but my satisfaction was a little damped when he added that the expense of the election would amount to about £2400, and that he thought it reasonable that we should share it between us. I paused, and recovering myself, hinted something of parental extravagance, and filial narrowness of circumstances and want of ready money… His answer was obliging, that he should be very much mortified if a few hundred pounds should prevent it, and that he had been afraid to offend me by offering it on less equal terms.

Gibbon offered to repay half after eight years. In 1776 the first volume of *Decline and Fall* was published, and was instantly a huge success. In 1779 he was apointed one of the Lords Commissioners of Trade and Planting, which brought him £7-800 p.a.

It must be allowed that our duty was not intolerably severe, and that I enjoyed many days and weeks of repose without being called away from my library to the office. My acceptance of a place provoked some of the leaders of the opposition with whom I had lived in intimacy; and I was most unjustly accused of deserting a party in which I had never been enlisted.

One of those critics was Mr Eliot. In 1781 Parliament was dissolved and Gibbon lost his Liskeard seat, because:

Mr Eliot was now deeply engaged in the measures of opposition, and the electors of Liskeard are commonly of the same opinion as Mr Eliot.

Quite. Lord North, the Prime Minister, found him a seat at Lymington but the disasters of the American War led to North's resignation. The Board of Trade was abolished and Gibbon lost his post. But the publication of volumes 2 and 3 of *Decline and Fall* were very lucrative. He continued as an MP through rumbustious times, but got no replacement sinecure despite voting with the government.

He could no longer afford to live in London, and retired to Lausanne, where he completed *Decline and Fall* in 1787, and then returned to London. Increasing ill health and corpulence made his last years miserable. He left an estate of £26,000.

Henry Brougham   1778-1868

Brougham is not now a well-known name, but in his time he was said by Macaulay to be the most popular man in England, excepting the King. He had three simultaneous careers, as a lawyer, a journalist and a politician, and all three were united by his huge ambition for both fame and money, and his formidable energy. He was also famous as an orator, and still holds the records for the longest speeches ever both in the Commons (over six hours) and the Lords (over three).

His family's estate was at Brougham Hall, just south of Carlisle, which he inherited, but at the time of his birth the family were living in Edinburgh, part of its intellectual elite. Brougham was a prodigy, who could read aged two. He was educated at Edinburgh High School and then the University, which was academically way ahead of Oxbridge at that time. Aged just 17, he sent papers to the Royal Society about experiments with light and colour: one of these might have kick-started photography if it had been published, but the Society rejected it as concerning art, not science.

Brougham qualified as an advocate in 1800, but he could get no paying briefs since the judges in Scotland were all Tories and hostile to even mildly liberal thought. Nor was there any chance of getting a Scottish seat in Westminster, as the Tories under Henry Dundas, Lord Melville, were in total control. Brougham was, however, one of the four founders in 1802 of the *Edinburgh Review*, a hugely successful quarterly publication which lasted until 1929, and was devastatingly frank in its liberal opinions. In 1803 he decided to move to London, and qualify in English law.

He wrote an important pamphlet against the slave trade, prior to a Bill which was accepted by the Commons but rejected by the Lords. He was engaged by Liverpool and Manchester (the latter having no MPs) to argue in Parliament against the newly introduced Orders in Council, which had enraged the USA, neutral in the war between Britain and France, and wrecked the cotton trade. He made a name for himself during three weeks there by his speeches, despite not being an MP.

In the *Edinburgh Review* he wrote a brave article praising the Spanish people, as opposed to their Lords and government, for resisting Napoleon. And he insisted that it was time British politicians, not least the Whigs, became more in touch with the people and allowed them their say.

Eventually, in 1810, the Duke of Bedford was persuaded to find him a seat at Camelford – which meant that as a radical he was in the unfortunate position of depending on a borough-monger for his place. He was also concerned that too much time in parliament, where MPs were unpaid, would cost him dearly in his career as a lawyer, for by this time he was earning an amazing £200 a day on the Northern Circuit. MPs supporting the government might get lucrative sinecures, but the Whigs were in opposition and so got none.

By the next election in 1812 the Duke had found someone who would pay proper money for the Camelford seat. Brougham was instead given a chance at Liverpool, always a contested election but where he was popular for ending the Orders in Council, which had been great for the cotton trade, though he was unpopular with Liverpool's slave traders: despite the trade's abolition some had continued, since the penalty was only a £20 fine; Brougham introduced a private member's bill, that slave trading be made a felony punishable by transportation. He fought an active campaign at Liverpool, but Tory cash and the influence of the Corporation defeated him.

While out of parliament he concentrated on the law, and also on introducing education for the working classes through the Lancasterian monitor system.

In 1815 he was given another pocket seat at Winchelsea. Whilst he was well known and popular outside parliament, and gave powerful speeches, within his own party he was becoming less popular: he seemed often to be promoting his own political interest, rather than that of the party or of the people, alarming the right wing by his demands for stronger policies, yet offending the radical wing with a defence of the 'interest' of the landed class. He ensured removal of income tax, which fell on the landed class, but did nothing against the taxes on food, including the Corn Laws. Over the next decade he would, within his party, become known as the 'Arch-fiend'.

In 1818 he did something extraordinary by standing for his home county, Westmorland. Its seats were controlled by the Earl of Lonsdale and had been uncontested for the previous 44 years. A Lonsdale job-ster named William Wordsworth wrote pamphlets (though not in verse) describing Brougham as 'a vile demagogue and democrat'.

Another poet, Byron, personally hated Brougham, and made these manuscript notes about him in 1818 – with Regency punctuation:

Distrusted by the democracy – disliked by the Whigs – and detested by the Tories – too much of a lawyer for the people – and too much of a demagogue for Parliament – a contestor of counties – and a candidate for cities – the refuse of half the electors of England – and representative at last upon sufferance of the proprietor of some rotten borough, which it would have been more independent to have purchased – a speaker upon all questions – and the outcast of all parties – his support has become alike formidable to all his enemies – (for he has no friends) and his vote can be only valuable when accompanied by his silence. – A disappointed man with a bad temper – he is endowed with considerable but not first-rate abilities – and has blundered on through life – remarkable only for a fluency, in which he has many rivals at the bar and in the Senate and an eloquence in which he has several superiors.

Brougham failed in Westmorland, but kept trying at later elections, with the Lowther family having to spend a fortune to keep him out – £40,000 in 1826! He was allowed back at Winchelsea.

Brougham's national popularity was hugely boosted by his becoming legal adviser to the Princess Caroline. She had married the future Prince Regent in 1795, probably against the wishes of both of them, but princes can't be choosers. The Prince discarded her a year later, and she was ignored by 'Society' but adored by the ordinary people, who hated the Prince.

When George III died in 1820, a bill was introduced to deprive her of the title Queen, as well as an attempt to divorce her on the grounds of adultery. There was massive public interest, with mobs in the streets. Brougham as her attorney made a two-day speech in her defence. The Lords passed the divorce bill, then swiftly withdrew it. Apparently Brougham knew, and perhaps had circulated the information, that the Prince, now George IV, had secretly married a Catholic prior to his marriage to Caroline: revealing a bigamous king would have created chaos!

Both inside and outside parliament Brougham was active in the expansion of Mechanics' Institutes, insisting that working men should form the majority on their management committees. He also started a Society for the Diffusion of Useful Knowledge, publishing cheap 32 page booklets. He wrote one himself, on hydrostatics, but it had to be withdrawn because of errors – typical of a man who oozed over-confidence. In January 1825 he started planning a secular university for London; the government would not support it, so University College initially had to be a private enterprise, backed by the Quaker banker Joseph Gurney and the Jewish 'bullion broker' Sir Isaac Goldsmid.

By 1825 Brougham was *de facto* leader of the opposition (there was no such formal role) but he did not inspire confidence. Some thought him mad. In 1830 the Tory government was finally defeated, having been in power since 1807. Before Lord Grey formed the next Whig government, Brougham told the house he was going to introduce a private electoral reform bill, even if neither of the main parties was prepared to do so. He spoke for the people – but was distrusted in Parliament, especially by his own party.

When George IV died, there had to be an election. The Winchelsea patron no longer backed him, so Brougham was first given a seat at Knaresborough, but then the publisher of the *Leeds Mercury* Edward Baines managed to get him nominated to stand for Yorkshire. It was only the fourth contested election there in 150 years, and Yorkshire was the most expensive electoral constituency in Britain. Brougham paid nothing himself, but won, his campaign being funded by dissenters and manufacturers. He promised the voters electoral reform and the abolition of slavery.

There was then a huge tug of war inside the Whig party, and within four months Brougham was forced to leave the Commons, accepting the role of Lord Chancellor and a peerage: it effectively ended his political career. As Lord Chancellor he managed, with difficulty, to get the Reform Bill through the Lords. By his hard work he also improved the Courts of Chancery, though some delays there would continue (the subject of Dickens' *Bleak House*).

By this time Brougham had lost his radical enthusiasm. He watered down the abolition of slavery by introducing a seven-year 'apprenticeship' rather than immediate emancipation, blocked educational reforms, blocked civil marriage and was responsible for the appalling 1834 Poor Law (workhouse or else starvation).

He meddled in the work of other government departments and leaked government business to the press. Some of his behaviour was quite crazy (taking the English Great Seal to Edinburgh and playing games with it, going to the races dressed in the Lord Chancellor's formal robes and wig) and he became a laughing stock. The Whigs were out of government in 1834, and that was also the end of Brougham as Lord Chancellor. Out of office he turned ultra-democrat, attacking the Whigs in his revenge.

It is questionable whether some of the MPs in this book were heroes or villains. In the case of Henry Brougham it is a lot simpler: he managed to be both, often simultaneously.